W9-CMZ-979

LIFE ON THE FRONT LINES

WORLD WAR I
ON THE FRONT LINES

by Tim Cooke

CAPSTONE PRESS
a capstone imprint

Edge Books are published by Capstone Press,
1710 Roe Crest Drive, North Mankato, Minnesota 56003
www.capstonepub.com

Published in 2014 by Capstone Publishers, Ltd.

Library of Congress Cataloging-in-Publication Data

Cooke, Tim, 1961-
 World War I on the front lines / by Tim Cooke.
     pages cm. -- (Edge books. Life on the front lines)
 Includes bibliographical references and index.
 Summary: "Approaches the topic of World War I the perspective of
soldiers fighting in it"-- Provided by publisher.
 Audience: Grades 4 to 6.
 ISBN 978-1-4914-0843-8 (library binding) -- ISBN 978-1-4914-0849-0
(pbk.)
 1. World War, 1914-1918--Trench warfare--Juvenile literature. 2.
Soldiers--United States--History--20th century--Juvenile
literature. I. Title.
 D522.7.C69 2015
 940.4--dc23

                     2013049459

For Brown Bear Books Ltd:
Editorial Director: Lindsey Lowe
Text: Tim Cooke
Children's Publisher: Anne O'Daly
Design Manager: Keith Davis
Designer: Lynne Lennon
Picture Manager: Sophie Mortimer
Production Director: Alastair Gourlay

Source Notes
p.9 Robert March Hanes, letter home dated September 10, 1917, from Docsouth.unc-edu/wwi/hanesletters, Selected letters 1917–1918 (no 4534); **p.11** Sam Avery, from *The Bridge of Sighs, Letters Home from A Yankee Doughboy 1916–1919*, www.worldwar1letters.wordpress.com; **p.15** Paul Maxwell, quoted in "Americans at War" by Jennifer D. Keene in *New Zealand's Great War*, edited by John Crawford and Ian McGibbon, Exisle Pub, 2007, p.120; **p.17** Roy Crowdy Avery, from Veterans History Project, memories of Roy C. Avery, June 1971, p.8, lcweb2.loc.gov/diglib/vhp/story/loc.natlib.afc2001001.00436/; **p.19** John C. Acker, quoted in *The War To End All Wars* by Edward M. Coffman, Oxford University Press, 1968, p.81; **p.21** Edward Lukert, quoted in *War Letters: Extraordinary Correspondence from American Wars* by Andrew Carroll, Simon & Schuster, 2002, p.157; **p.25** Lewis C Plush, quoted in *War Letters: Extraordinary Correspondence from American Wars* by Andrew Carroll, Simon & Schuster, 2002, p.167; **p.27** Lloyd Brewer Palmer, letter home, November 15, 1918, from www.pbs.org/wgbh/americanexperience/features/general-article/warletters-letters/; **p.29** Frances J. Gulick, quoted in *American Legion Monthly*, February 1930 issue.

Photo Credits
Front Cover: Robert Hunt Library
Interior: All images Robert Hunt Library
Artistic effects: Shutterstock

Printed in China

TABLE OF CONTENTS

WORLD WAR I

After the **assassination** of Archduke Franz Ferdinand of Austria in June 1914, Austria-Hungary declared war on Serbia. It blamed the Serbs for the killing. A series of **ultimatums** and **alliances** eventually drew most of Europe into war. The Central Powers included Austria–Hungary, Germany, and Turkey. They fought the Allies, which included Great Britain, France, and Russia.

Heavily burdened U.S. troops go into battle at the Battle of Cantigny in France in May 1918. The battle was the first U.S. attack in the war.

After a German advance into northern France in August 1914, the Western Front stalled. Millions of troops faced one another in man-made ditches called trenches, sometimes only a few dozen yards apart. There was also fighting on the Eastern Front and in Turkey. German submarines attacked ships in the Atlantic Ocean. After Americans died on U.S. and other ships, the United States entered the war in April 1917 on the side of the Allies. Some 2 million U.S. soldiers served on the Western Front before Germany surrendered to the Allies in November 1918.

U.S. soldiers enjoy a meal at a camp in France. Living conditions were far better in rear areas than in the front-line trenches facing the enemy.

- **assassination:** a murder carried out for political reasons

- **ultimatum:** a demand from one country to another which, if it is not met, will lead to war

- **alliance:** an agreement between countries to support one another in international affairs

CHAPTER 1

THE MAKING OF A SOLDIER

Trench warfare required millions of troops. All the major combatants had to dramatically increase the size of their armies. When the United States joined the war, its army numbered just 300,000 soldiers. This was not enough to make a big impact in the fighting. U.S. president Woodrow Wilson realized that the army might not get enough recruits if it relied on volunteers. In May 1917 he signed the Selective Services Act into law. It introduced a draft. Men could then be forced to serve in the military.

Uncle Sam rolls up his sleeves ready to fight in this recruiting poster for the U.S. Army.

A huge **propaganda** campaign was launched to convince reluctant Americans of the importance of winning the war in Europe.

U.S. soldiers were known as "doughboys," which had been a nickname for U.S. soldiers since the 1840s. They were drafted from all walks of life. At its peak, the American Expeditionary Forces (AEF) had 2 million troops in Europe.

Doughboys train with bayonets in France. Bayonets were attached to rifles for hand-to-hand fighting in the trenches.

RECRUITMENT AND TRAINING

The U.S. Army that was sent to Europe was a mixture of volunteers and conscripts recruited through a draft. All recruits were sent to training camps. The camps were still being built when the first men arrived. Basic training lasted three months. Recruits learned how to fight at close range and handle their weapons. Constant **drills** improved their fitness.

An official picks a number as part of the U.S. draft. Men who were drafted had no choice but to serve in the war.

A U.S. Army recruit (left) is timed during a test. His task is to fit wooden shapes into holes in a board.

U.S. troops build a structure during a training exercise at their base in France in early 1918. Such exercises taught units to work as a team.

● **drill:** a repeated series of movements that soldiers practice until they become second nature

TRANSPORTATION

For U.S. soldiers World War I began as they boarded ships. Millions of men had to be shipped to Europe. Troop ships sailed in convoys. Warships escorted the convoys to protect them from German submarines. About 18,653 ships made the voyage successfully. In Europe troops traveled by railroad, truck, or even taxi. But soldiers also had to march long distances to get into position to fight.

U.S. troops line up after landing in France. For many soldiers the war was the first time they had traveled abroad.

British and French troops travel in buses and trucks. In 1914 the French Army hired a fleet of taxi cabs to move soldiers to defend Paris.

U.S. Marines wave as their troop train leaves for the front in June 1917. Most U.S. troops arrived in France in good spirits.

CHAPTER 2

AT THE FRONT

By early 1915, the Western Front stretched for 440 miles (708 km), from the North Sea to Switzerland. The front was made up of two parallel sets of trenches, dug-outs, and barbed-wire obstacles separated by an area known as no–man's–land. The trenches were built in a series of zigzags to make it harder for any invading attackers to fire straight along them.

In 1917 the first U.S. arrivals joined British and French units already in the trenches. Only 40 percent of troops fought at any one time. The other 60 percent were resting behind the lines or helping to support the front-line troops.

A British lieutenant uses a foot pump to try to clear water from a trench. Constantly having wet feet caused a painful condition called trench foot.

In the front trenches, soldiers spent long periods waiting to fight. Soldiers were warned of incoming artillery shells by the high-pitched scream they made. In the case of an attack, men went "over the top." They climbed out of the trenches and charged toward the enemy through mud, barbed wire, and machine-gun fire and shelling.

A German firing squad takes aim at a spy. Spies on both sides faced almost certain death if they were caught.

LIVING CONDITIONS

There was little comfort in the trenches. They were often full of standing water and running with rats. Soldiers wore the same clothes for weeks, and they were often short on food and water. They built underground **bunkers** where they could sleep. They lived on canned corned beef called "monkey-meat," bacon, and hardtack, which is a kind of dry biscuit.

German soldiers relax in their bunker. Deep underground, bunkers could offer some protection from artillery attack.

British troops enjoy hot stew in a trench near Cambrai, France, in winter 1917. Hot food was a luxury in the front lines, where cooking fires could attract enemy fire.

A British soldier washes in a flooded shell hole. Men could go for days without washing, and rarely had any hot water.

● **bunker:** a fortified underground shelter

UNIFORMS AND EQUIPMENT

The huge numbers of new U.S. recruits meant that uniforms and equipment were often in short supply. Soldiers were issued khaki coats. The coarse wool was lined with cotton to prevent itching. Soldiers wound **puttees** around their ankles to stop mud from getting into their leather boots. Many U.S. soldiers used British or French helmets and gas masks. The U.S. Army commander, General John Pershing, believed the rifle was the key weapon in the war. U.S. soldiers used Springfield or M1917 rifles.

This German soldier wears the distinctive pointed pickelhaube helmet. The helmet was part of the traditional uniform of the German state of Prussia.

U.S. soldiers and their French allies (right) discuss the performance of their respective rifles. Most American infantry used the highly reliable Springfield rifle.

● **puttee:** a tape wound around the lower leg for protection

MEDICINE AND HEALTH

More U.S. soldiers died from disease and accidents than from wounds. Contagious diseases were a big problem in the camps. Despite being **vaccinated** for some diseases before they sailed for Europe, many soldiers died from diseases such as measles, mumps, smallpox, meningitis, typhoid, and diptheria. Camp cleanliness was improved to cut down on the death rate, but in September 1918 an outbreak of "Spanish flu" struck both sides. Up to 40 percent of U.S. Navy sailors had the disease in 1918.

Wounded men wait to be loaded onto a hospital train after the Battle of Cambrai in 1917.

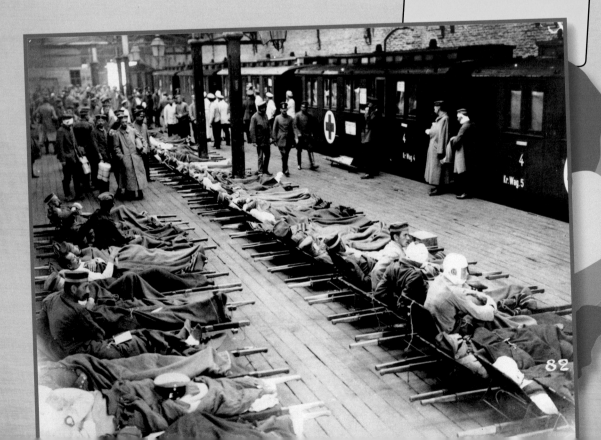

EYEWITNESS

NAME: John C. Acker
RANK: Sergeant, 107th Ammunition Train, 32nd Division
PLACE: Northern France

" Had the Spanish 'flu.' It hits suddenly and one's temperature nearly chases the mercury out thru' the top of the MD's thermometer. "

Ambulancemen evacuate soldiers suffering from trench foot in 1916. The condition caused painful swelling of the feet.

● **vaccinate:** to inject someone with a vaccine to provide protection from getting an infectious disease

19

UNDER FIRE

Trenches were subject to shelling. But when soldiers left their trenches, they also faced enemy guns. For most of the time, both sides remained in their trenches. Before an attack, a **barrage** of artillery shells pounded enemy positions. Then whistles blew, and the infantry went "over the top." If the barrage didn't work, enemy machine guns opened up as the men left their trenches. It was rare for either side to reach enemy lines. If they did, they tried to drive the occupants out and take control of the trench.

U.S. troops prepare to defend a section of the front line in France. They are ready to open fire on German attackers.

A U.S. machine-gun platoon advances cautiously through woods during an offensive near Argonne, France, in October 1918.

EYEWITNESS

NAME: Edward Lukert
UNIT: 1st Lieutenant,
5th Division
PLACE: Northern France

"We were all subjected to several different kinds of [gas] today, with and without masks, and as usual, I cannot rid my clothes of the odor. It is sure awful stuff ... Deadly and usually insures a slow horrible death."

Poison gas drifts across the front during an attack in 1917. Gas was used by both sides. It was released to be carried by the wind over the enemy trenches. The gas affected the lungs, often causing a slow and painful death.

● **barrage:** a heavy bombardment of artillery fire that often moves ahead of advancing infantry

CHAPTER 3

SPIRIT AND MORALE

Trench warfare was not only uncomfortable, but also terrifying. It sapped the **morale** of soldiers on all sides. When the United States entered World War I in 1917, morale among its European allies was low. The arrival of hundreds of thousands of U.S. troops in Europe boosted their spirits. For their part, many of the American soldiers believed strongly that they were fighting to preserve democracy. A propaganda campaign in the U.S. training camps had persuaded U.S. soldiers that it was important to defeat the Germans.

An African-American soldier takes a break during a gas-mask drill.

British troops in Greece play soccer to celebrate Christmas Day in 1915. Sports were a favorite way to relax away from the front.

Having a strong sense of purpose helped keep up soldiers' spirits in the appalling conditions of the trenches. But it was still very difficult for soldiers to remain cheerful on a daily basis. They suffered from boredom, sickness, cold, uncomfortable living conditions, and lack of food and sleep. There was a constant fear of artillery and infantry attack. Attacks seemed to cost many lives for little military benefit. Many soldiers had to work really hard to prevent their spirits from sinking too low.

● **morale:** the fighting spirit of a person or group

FRIENDSHIP AND CAMARADERIE

Stuck in the trenches, soldiers made firm friendships as they played cards, chatted, and even picked lice off each other. The shared experience of war encouraged a strong sense of **camaraderie** among troops. Armies were arranged in small units that encouraged soldiers to be loyal to one another. Some U.S. soldiers also made close connections with the French. Some married French women, while others made long lasting friendships with the French families in whose homes they stayed.

A U.S. soldier makes friends with French children in Brancourt, which U.S. forces captured from the Germans in October 1918.

● **camaraderie:** a spirit of comradeship and trust between friends or colleagues

British gunners in northern France in November 1916 wrapped themselves in sheepskins and furs for warmth.

U.S. troops pose for the camera in front of a tent in France in September 1917.

LETTERS AND DIARIES

Writing home and receiving letters was a lifeline for soldiers. Every week around 12.5 million letters were delivered to soldiers at the front. All letters home were **censored**. Military censors removed or crossed out any information that might be useful to the enemy if the letter was captured. They also looked for signs of poor morale. Many soldiers also kept diaries. They used them to record their true feelings. If they were killed, they wanted their families to know what the war had really been like.

British soldiers in Greece catch up on the latest news. Armies often produced their own newspapers for troops.

A British captain writes in his diary in February 1915.

EYEWITNESS

NAME: Lloyd Brewer Palmer
UNIT: U.S. Army, France
PLACE: Northern France, November 11, 1918, **Armistice** Day

" At 10:45 [a.m.] the order came to cease firing ... That was absolutely the happiest moment of my life. "

British soldiers write home.

- **censor:** to examine letters and remove sensitive details

- **Armistice:** an agreement to stop fighting a war; the WWI armistice was made at about 11:00 a.m. on November 11, 1918

RECREATION

The Young Men's Christian Association (YMCA) was in charge of the U.S. recreation program in France. It built YMCA huts where soldiers could watch movies, play pool, listen to music, or write letters. The "Y" built a total of 952 huts. It also produced a newspaper for soldiers. Every four months, a soldier had a seven-day leave. The YMCA ran tours for soldiers to visit Paris or to stay at YMCA resorts.

Men from a British Ordnance company take time out to play cards on top of the pile of mortar shells into which they were inserting fuses.

U.S. soldiers read in the library at a YMCA hut in France.

U.S. soldiers enjoy an impromptu piano recital in the ruins of a church that had been destroyed in the fighting.

GLOSSARY

alliance (uh-LYE-anz)—an agreement between countries to support one another in international affairs

Armistice (AR-miss-tiss)—an agreement to stop fighting a war; the WWI armistice was made at about 11:00 a.m. on November 11, 1918

artillery (ar-TILL-uh-ree)—large weapons, such as cannon and mortars

assassination (uh-sass-uh-NAY-shun)—a murder carried out for political reasons

barrage (buh-RAHZH)—a heavy bombardment of artillery fire that often moves ahead of advancing infantry

bunker (bun-KER)—a fortified underground shelter

camaraderie (cam-ah-RAH-der-ee)—a spirit of comradeship and trust between friends or colleagues

censor (SEN-ser)—to examine correspondence and remove or cross out sensitive information

conscript (con-SKRIPT)—to force people to join the armed services

draft (DRAFT)—the process of selecting individuals to serve in the military

drill (DRIL)—a repeated series of movements that soldiers practice until they become second nature

khaki (KAH-kee)—a tough cloth of a yellow-brown color

morale (muh-RAL)—the fighting spirit of a person or group, and how confident he or they feel of winning a victory

propaganda (prop-uh-GAN-duh)—material that is produced to convince people that a view or side is right or that another is wrong

puttee (puh-TEE)—a tape wound around the lower leg for protection

ultimatum (uhl-tuh-MAY-tuhm)—a demand from one country to another which, if it is not met, will lead to war

vaccinate (vak-suh-NAYT)—to inject someone with a vaccine to protect him or her from getting an infectious disease

READ MORE

Barber, Nicola. *World War I*. Living Through. Chicago, Ill.: Heinemann-Raintree, 2012.

Gregory, Josh. *World War I*. Cornerstones of Freedom. New York: Children's Press, 2012.

Lewis, John E. *On the Front Line: True World War I Stories*. London: Constable, 2013.

Samuels, Charlie. *Machines and Weaponry of World War I*. Machines that Won the War. New York: Gareth Stevens Publishing, 2013.

Samuels, Charlie. *Timeline of World War I*. Americans at War. New York: Gareth Stevens Publishing, 2011.

INTERNET SITES

FactHound offers a safe, fun way to find Internet sites related to this book. All of the sites on FactHound have been researched by our staff.

Here's all you do:

Visit www.facthound.com

Type in this code: 9781491408438

Super-cool stuff!

Check out projects, games and lots more at
www.capstonekids.com

INDEX